It's been said that Seattle, like Rome, is defined by seven hills. A stretch perhaps, but in the 15 years I've lived here, I've witnessed a dizzying number of events that have helped shape this town. The streets ran untamed during WTO protests in 1999. The city survived the first dot-com bubble – and its inevitable bust. If that didn't shake us, Seattleites felt our very foundation literally crack during the 6.8 magnitude Nisqually earthquake of 2001.

Though things have felt more settled lately, change is still afoot. As Microsoft reaches middle age, Amazon is spurring explosive growth and has triggered a second tech boom, which has brought new life to town. Restaurants and shops seem to open at a daily clip, and the downtown waterfront is going through an expansive renovation, providing more parks and paths, and access to Elliott Bay.

Change is good. Seattle is still young, and defining itself every day.

---

the hunt seattle writer

jenise silva

Jenise is a writer and photographer who has eaten her way through every state and many foreign lands in the course of her work and play. She's contributed to *Eater*, *Seattlest*, *Seattle Refined* and *Travel Sages*, among others. You can usually find her pursuing her passions (food, film, farming, philanthropy, travel and the arts) – sometimes all at once – in the beautiful Pacific Northwest.

ACE HOTEL

ACE HOTEL

Trendy and affordable boarding house

2423 1st Avenue (near Wall Street; Belltown)
+1 206 448 4721 / acehotel.com

Double from $129

Ace Hotel screams Pacific Northwest. From the hardwood floors to the
loft ceilings, Ace has been making visitors feel right at home since 1999.
Minimal yet luxurious, this hotel reclaimed and updated a former maritime
workers' dwellings with a mix of sleek vintage and locally made furnishings
in the lobby, and uncluttered yet comfy quarters that feature artwork by
Shepard Fairey and KAWS. One thing to note is that most rooms share
a bathroom in the hallway, but there are a few with en suites available.
A stone's throw from the Seattle waterfront and dog-friendly,
this is a steal for those in the know.

HOTEL MAX

HOTEL MAX

Centrally located with artistic flair

620 Stewart Street (near 7th Avenue; Downtown)
+1 206 728 6299 / hotelmaxseattle.com

Double from $179

Tapping into the energy of the city, Hotel Max speaks to the creative spirit in all of us: the lobby is awash in original art. The accommodation even boasts an entire floor that pays homage to the Sub Pop indie music label, where the rooms include record players and a selection of vinyl to suit almost any taste. There's complimentary coffee, a craft beer happy hour held daily and the unique amenities include a pillow menu and a library of faith-based books that cater to your spiritual needs. Bring your pooch along, too – they'll love it.

HOTEL SORRENTO

Grand hotel full of activity

900 Madison Street (near Terry Avenue; Downtown)
+1 206 622 6400 / hotelsorrento.com

Double from $299

As the oldest boutique stay in Seattle, the Sorrento sits high on a corner near Downtown, and is surrounded by myriad cultural activities. The lobby's Fireside Room, replete with leather club chairs and plush sofas flanking the Rookwood Pottery fireplace, is a stunner. The guest rooms are nothing short of refined elegance with high-quality Egyptian cotton sheets, goose down pillows and bathrooms outfitted with Venetian marble. But the pampering doesn't stop there: you'll also receive a shoe shine, French press coffee and have access to on-site services such as Shiatsu massage and a hair salon. Start your night in the Dunbar Room with a killer cocktail before heading out to see what Seattle has to offer.

INN AT THE MARKET

Slumber above the action

86 Pine Street (near 1st Avenue; Downtown)
+1 206 443 3600 / innatthemarket.com

Double from $350

Just steps from Pike Place Market, Inn at the Market has become a mainstay for travelers who are looking to be in the heart of the city yet tucked away in quiet reverie. Stylish, remodeled rooms are outfitted with Hypnos mattresses, Sferra linens and plush bathrobes, and sport floor-to-ceiling windows with unparalleled views of the Market and mountains. Stay out late, wake up early and enjoy the sight of Washington State ferries crossing Elliott Bay as you tuck into breakfast in bed.

PANAMA HOTEL

Memorable lodging

605 1/2 South Main Street (near 6th Avenue South; International District)
+1 206 223 9242 / panamahotelseattle.com

Double from $130

Looking for a little history? Panama Hotel has it in spades. Originally built in 1910 as a hotel that served primarily Japanese immigrants, the Panama was the hub for Seattle's Japantown. This is a time capsule, and was recently designated a National Historic Landmark. A sobering note of interest here is the glass panes in the floors that allow visitors a view into the basement, where luggage covered in travel stickers – left behind by those who were sent to internment camps in the 1940s – is still stored. Guest rooms here are a tad small, but they're certainly big on character as they're decorated with pre-War furniture. If you're thinking about skipping the tea room, don't; it's definitely worth an afternoon visit.

THOMPSON SEATTLE

Urban digs

110 Stewart Street (near 1st Avenue; Downtown)
+1 206 623 4600 / thompsonhotels.com

Double from $419

This town upped its hotel game with the opening of
Thompson Seattle. Commanding a corner that is part Downtown,
part Belltown, this 158-room luxury property is a stellar jumping-off point
for a stay in The Emerald City. Designed with a nod to its magnificent
surroundings of Puget Sound and the Olympic Mountains beyond, you may
never want to leave your room. That said, do head to the restaurant, Scout,
and the stunning rooftop bar, The Nest.

THOMPSON SEATTLE

capitol hill

Veer a few blocks off the Pike-Pine Corridor
down 14th Avenue East and you'll see Capitol Hill —
my homebase when I first moved here — in all its
grand glory. Better known as "Millionaire's Row,"
impressive early-20th-century homes line the street
adjacent to Volunteer Park, the highest point, providing
great views of the surrounding mountains. In the
heart of the hood, bars, restaurants, coffee shops and
music venues vie for attention, but if it's fresh air you
crave, claim some space at nearby Cal Anderson Park,
where you'll find Frisbee-chasing dogs and a laid-back
vibe. This has also long been the center of the LGBTQ
community, though some fear that's changing as new
development chips away at the counterculture fabric.
Change may be in the air, but the true spirit of
Capitol Hill continues to thrive.

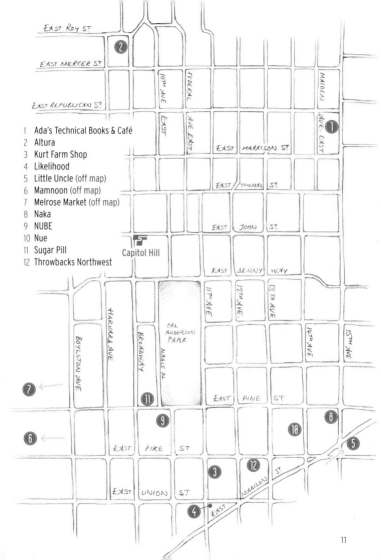

EAST ROY ST

EAST MERCER ST.

EAST REPUBLICAN ST.

10TH AVE EAST

FEDERAL AVE EAST

EAST HARRISON ST

MALDEN AVE EAST

EAST THOMAS ST

EAST JOHN ST

EAST DENNY WAY

1 Ada's Technical Books & Café
2 Altura
3 Kurt Farm Shop
4 Likelihood
5 Little Uncle (off map)
6 Mamnoon (off map)
7 Melrose Market (off map)
8 Naka
9 NUBE
10 Nue
11 Sugar Pill
12 Throwbacks Northwest

Capitol Hill

BOYLSTON AVE

HARVARD AVE

BROADWAY

CAL ANDERSON PARK

NAGLE PL

11TH AVE

12TH AVE

13TH AVE

14TH AVE

15TH AVE

EAST PINE ST

EAST PIKE ST

EAST UNION ST

MADISON ST

EAST

ADA'S TECHNICAL BOOKS & CAFÉ

Geek central

425 15th Avenue East (near East Republican Street)
+1 206 322 1058 / seattletechnicalbooks.com / Open daily

Ever wanted to know how you go about building a near-functioning rocket ship in your own backyard? I quickly found out when I attended a reading at Ada's Technical Books & Café. If, like me, you delight in the inner workings of just about anything, you could easily get lost in Ada's for days. Whether it's learning how to build a civilization in the aftermath of a cataclysm or how to tackle the afterlife with science, the books lining the walls here hold all of the answers, and a snack from the café (the rustic grilled cheese made with Beecher's on sourdough is solid) will give you the energy to spend the day absorbing as much knowledge as you can. STEM students definitely welcome.

ALTURA

Elegant Italian eatery

617 Broadway East (near East Roy Street) / +1 206 402 6749
alturarestaurant.com / Closed Sunday and Monday

Dinner in this modern age can sometimes devolve into a rushed affair that consists of grabbing a quick bite before heading off to your next obligation. But sometimes you just have to say "enough is enough," and make dinner your only plan for the night. When I'm in the mood to linger over my meal, I head to Altura, where there's no need to fret over what to order – just sit back, relax and let chef Nathan Lockwood guide you over the next several hours through his Italian tasting menu of pure dining bliss. All things fresh and foraged, like Saltspring Island mussels, Perigord black truffles and fettuccine dusted with Sardinian cured tuna heart, await. Definitely worth taking the time to savor.

KURT FARM SHOP

Dairy lover's dream

1424 11th Avenue (near East Pike Street) / No phone
kurtwoodfarms.com / Open daily

While visiting Kurt Timmermeister on his Vashon Island farm, I was delighted to meet his Jersey cow, Dinah – the namesake behind the amazing cheeses Kurt produces. His offerings were once confined to intimate dinners at his place, but he soon brought the farm-to-table treats into the city. His recent outpost, Kurt Farm Shop at Chophouse Row, is a slice of pastoral paradise where fans line up for his frozen goodies laced with flavors like Triple Crown blackberries, lemon verbena and bay laurel – all ingredients grown on his property. You can also pick up his *New York Times*-heralded Dinah cheese – a rich, buttery, Camembert-style fromage – while you're there.

LIKELIHOOD

Hip sneaks

1101 East Union Street (at 11th Avenue) / +1 206 257 0577
likelihood.us / Closed Monday

Finally, sneakers get the respect they deserve at this modern boutique featuring all things fashionable for the foot. Although it's men's footwear only, that doesn't stop me from dropping by anytime I'm in the vicinity to check out their latest merchandise, not to mention their amazing shop dog, Kevin. The store's build-out is as sleek as the shoes themselves, and is a fitting place to highlight the latest and freshest by all of the major designers. Kicks, trainers, Chucks... it doesn't matter what you call 'em, Likelihood will undoubtedly have the hookup for the sneakerhead in your life.

LITTLE UNCLE

Authentic Thai nosh

**1523 East Madison Street #101
(near 16th Avenue) / +1 206 549 6507
littleuncleseattle.com / Closed Sunday
and Monday**

During my travels abroad, some of my
most memorable experiences have come
from rubbing elbows with locals while
tucking into the nosh from street food
vendors. I've not been to Thailand yet,
so until then I make it a point to stop by
and visit the chefs and friendly owners at
Little Uncle. This bustling eating house
dishes up Thai takeaway, but if you want
to hang out with Seattleites, nudge your
way to a table or the stand-up counter.
Chefs PK and Wiley are always present,
serving up the classics, like fried noodles
with fresh tofu sautéed with garlic, chili
and basil, and Chiang Mai chicken curry
made with coconut milk, red curry paste,
fried shallots, ginger, sprouts and house-
pickled Chinese mustard.

mamnoon

Contemporary Middle Eastern fare

1508 Melrose Avenue (near Minor Avenue) / **+1 206 906 9606**
mamnoonrestaurant.com / Open daily

On one of my earliest visits to Mamnoon, Barbara Massaad – the renowned
food historian and early consultant for this eatery – gave a group of us
some lessons she'd shared with the chef on how she made manaeesh
(dough topped with thyme, cheese and meat) and the lovely pita that now
graces many of the Lebanese and Syrian plates here. Today, executive chef
Jason Stratton is building on those influences with great success. I usually
gravitate toward the muhammara, a savory mezze featuring walnuts,
pepper paste and pomegranate, and the lamb kefta off the grill. The tahini
ice cream sandwich – made with two brownie cookies and garnished with
crunchy almonds – is an exemplary capper.

MELROSE MARKET

A local destination for dining and shopping

1531 Melrose Avenue (near Pine Street) / No phone
melrosemarketseattle.com / Open daily

In Capitol Hill, there's one marketplace where every single business is just so right that I wanted to include all of them in this guide. For brevity's sake, I'll highlight them here. In need of the ultimate housewarming gift? Hit up Glasswing for the Mason jar cocktail shaker set or Butter Home for hand-dyed shibori kitchen towels. In the market for a full-service butchery? Make your way to Rain Shadow Meats. Trying to find a showstopping bouquet of seasonal, organic flowers? Marigold & Mint is the place. Hungry for lingcod with roasted turnips? Take a seat at Sitka & Spruce. What I'm saying is, go to Melrose Market. There's plenty more, for sure – once you step foot inside, it's almost impossible to leave.

NAKA

Modern eats from Japan

1449 East Pine Street (near 15th Avenue) / +1 206 294 5230
nakaseattle.com / Closed Monday and Tuesday

When was the last time you witnessed a Japanese snowfall? For me,
it was a couple of years ago – but it wasn't in Japan. It was when I saw
chef Shota Nakajima compete in Seattle's first Itadakimasu Day,
a cooking competition to recognize the mastery of chefs outside of Japan.
Nakajima's dish was a brilliant interpretation (intricately sliced bamboo leaf,
daikon and lotus root, and marinated black cod and sea urchin), and it won
him the competition. Seattle was also a winner when Nakajima opened his
dining establishment, Naka. Based on kaiseki, a traditional, multi-course
Japanese dinner, plate after plate of astounding creations, like tuna aemono
with uni and grilled black cod with corn tempura, is served up. Let it snow!

NUBE

Green goodies

1527 10th Avenue (near East Pine Street) / +1 206 402 4515
nubegreen.com / Open daily

Sometimes we do things not because we necessarily want to, but because we think it's good for us (CrossFit, anyone?). Then there are times when the things we love to do (like shop) benefit not only us, but others, too. So do yourself a favor and head to NUBE. In addition to scoring some fashionable threads and must-have housewares, you'll also be helping out Mother Nature. NUBE exclusively sources products that are recycled, upcycled, reclaimed or reworked. Plus, they're all made in the United States, making your new purchases eco-friendly and economically sustainable. Who knew shopping could be such a good thing?

NUE

Global flavors

1519 14th Avenue (near East Pine Street)
+1 206 257 0312 / nueseattle.com
Open daily

Nue is my ideal restaurant concept.
There's no pretense, no need for labels,
just amazing food. Owner and chef-
patron Chris Cvetkovich simply wants to
share with you the soul-warming nosh
he has experienced around the world.
When I first met Chris, his travel tales and
enthusiasm for international cuisine were
infectious. When you're here, you can enjoy
housemade Vietnamese pepper and sweet
beef jerky, rich Malaysian seafood curry or
fluffy Brazilian fritters made from peeled
black-eyed peas. Nue is a phenomenal
place to do a little table-side traveling if
you're feeling the itch for a trip but don't
have the time to jet off.

SUGAR PILL

Just what the doctor ordered

900 East Pine Street (near Broadway) / +1 206 322 7455
sugarpillseattle.com / Open daily

Have you ever had the experience of walking out of a medical office, excited to have script in hand but dreading the trip to your drab and dreary pharmacy? I'm not an M.D., but if I were I would only prescribe items that could be dispensed by the apothecary at Sugar Pill, whose aim is to highlight the medicinal properties of foodstuffs: local honey for your tea, sea salt and chocolate for your tummy, and, of course, some exotic bitters – which got their start as a digestion aid – for a sensational Manhattan. Don't get me wrong: you don't need to be sick to enjoy the mysterious and comforting wonders of this place. Simply walking into Sugar Pill is guaranteed to elevate your mood.

THROWBACKS NORTHWEST

One-of-a-kind sportswear

1205 East Pike Street, Suite 1D (near 12th Avenue) / +1 206 402 4855
throwbacksnw.com / Open daily

Looking to impress the sports lover in your life? Then step into the time machine that is Throwbacks Northwest and take a ride back to the good ol' days when pro athletes played for nothing more than the love of the game. With its retro gear, including jerseys (some signed), apparel and trading cards, this place is one big nostalgia fest. It turns out you don't even need to be a sports fan to crave this stuff. These iconic symbols from the past seem to have seeped into all of our psyches. Heck, I even felt a twinge of homesickness for the Cubbies. They'll win it one of these years, right?

baker's dozen

Early to rise

Sweet or savory? This city is blessed with hardworking, award-winning bakers who get up before the sun to make sure you have the pastries you need to start the day off right. God bless 'em.

A lovely micro-bakery in Capitol Hill's equally lovely Chophouse Row, **Amandine Bakeshop** is classic in its technique, and you'll be hard-pressed to find a better macaron Gerbet around. The croissants and cakes also tempt the senses. If you're free on a Saturday, stop by, grab a treat and lounge to the beats of DJ Bean One.

Bakery Nouveau is where anyone serious about seeking out the finest in baked goods eventually ends up. From the moment you walk into this French bakery, you know they mean business. Line up in front of the long glass display case and set your sights on the quiches, pizzas, cakes and other wonders they have created just for you. You can't go wrong with a cherry, almond and pear tart or the twice-baked croissant.

Another Capitol Hill gem is this tiny and exquisite patisserie. Get to James Beard semifinalist Neil Robertson's **Crumble & Flake Patisserie** early to make sure you walk away with one of their crusty croissants. They do traditional French treats beautifully, but if you're in a playful mood, there's always the Cheweo, an Oreo-inspired cookie made with a pure butter filling.

Coyle's Bakeshop is an appealing little sun-soaked shop in Greenwood, where you can pick up one of their flaky cretzels (a croissant-pretzel hybrid) or filling quiches – if they've yet to sell out – stuffed with seasonal ingredients. I always find a slice of the chocolate cake equally irresistible.

The neon sign calling out **Columbia City Bakery** is a beacon for lovers of confections. A popular hang, the bakery satisfies all different cravings – from a perfectly scored pain de campagne to a savory slice of torta rustica. For the sweet tooth, the profiteroles rule.

AMANDINE BAKESHOP
1424 11th Avenue (near East Pike Street; Capitol Hill)
+1 206 948 2097, amandineseattle.com, open daily

BAKERY NOUVEAU
137 15th Avenue East (near East John Court; Capitol Hill)
+1 206 858 6957, bakerynouveau.com, open daily

COLUMBIA CITY BAKERY
4865 Rainier Avenue South
(near South Ferdinand Street; Columbia City)
+1 206 723 6023, columbiacitybakery.com, open daily

COYLE'S BAKESHOP
8300 Greenwood Avenue North (at North 83rd Street;
Greenwood), +1 206 257 4736, coylesbakeshop.com
open daily

CRUMBLE & FLAKE PATISSERIE
1500 East Olive Way (at East Howell Street;
Capitol Hill), +1 206 329 1804, crumbleandflake.com
closed Monday and Tuesday

CRUMBLE & FLAKE PATISSERIE

fremont

eastlake, wallingford

———••———

So named because of its proximity to Lake Union,
Eastlake is surrounded by houseboats, kayakers and
dock dogs, is close to the University District but far enough
away that it isn't filled with college students, and was
made famous by rom-com *Sleepless in Seattle*. A spot
I love here is a cute pocket park that hugs the shore of the
lake, conveniently across the street from Pete's Wine Shop.
Nearby Wallingford, located on the lake's north shore, is a
terrific place for taking in views of the Olympic and Cascade
mountain ranges, and is home to the ever-popular, original
Dick's Drive-In. It also has the distinction of abutting the
"Center of the Universe" – Fremont. Self-proclaimed as
such by its residents, this community is known for its zany
landmarks, like the salvaged statue of Vladimir Lenin
and the 18-foot troll sculpture that lives under the
Aurora Bridge. Every summer, the naked bike riders come
out in droves for the annual Solstice Parade. Quirky, indeed.

1 Book Larder
2 Café Turko
3 Manolin
4 Pomerol
5 Recycled Cycles
6 Revel
7 Sushi Kappo Tamura
8 Ten22home
9 Uneeda Burger
10 Westward

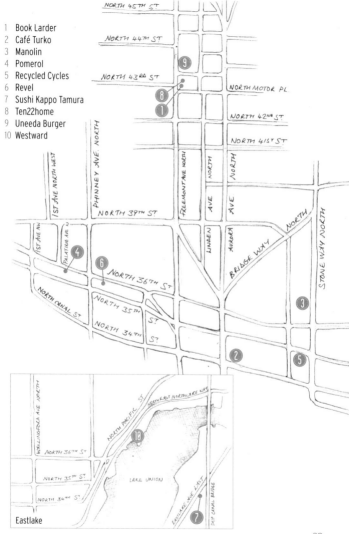

Eastlake

BOOK LARDER

A cookbook lover's playground

4252 Fremont Avenue North (near North Motor Place)
+1 206 397 4271 / booklarder.com / Open daily

I can't quite place my finger on why I'm so crazy about cookbooks — maybe it's the captivating photos, or the elaborate recipes, or the tales recounted within. Do you share a similar sense of culinary obsession? Do you have years' worth of cooking titles stacked in your kitchen and feel like you could use a few more? If so, head over to Book Larder, where they'll have everything to feed your fix. Thousands of tantalizing volumes from noted chefs and food pros line the walls. You can also get up close and personal with your most-loved scribes at the store's author chats, cooking classes and book signings throughout the year.

CAFÉ TURKO

Flavors of Turkey

900 North 34th Street (near Aurora Avenue North)
+1 206 284 9954 / cafe-turko.com / Open daily

When I last stopped by Café Turko, co-owner Süreyya Gökeri was busy in the garden, snipping herbs that would soon finish off the savory Cappadocia chicken köftes served at her delightful eatery. Always quick with a smile and a story, Süreyya stopped by my table to say hello and drop off a sprig of her newly cut herbs, also letting me know my freshly brewed Turkish tea and sucuk (spiced Halal beef sausages) plate was on its way. That was fine by me. Once I'm nestled into this charming alcove surrounded by luxurious handmade rugs and other imports from Turkey, all is right with the world.

MANOLIN

Expertly prepared seafood

3621 Stone Way North (near North 36th Street)
+1 206 294 3331 / manolinseattle.com / Closed Monday

When Manolin was named one of America's top restaurants by *Bon Appétit* magazine, the subsequent foodie ferver was astounding. Fortunately, my initial visits were prior to the well-deserved buzz, when it was easier to snag a seat at this tastefully decorated, nautical-themed establishment. Finding an open table may have become more of a sport, but that doesn't stop me from pointing anyone within sight in the direction of Manolin for a terrific meal and impeccable service. Their whole branzino (European sea bass) is definitely of the sea, and don't even think about passing on the succulent squid fired on the grill.

POMEROL

Delectable French cuisine

127 North 36th Street (near Palatine Avenue North)
+1 206 632 0135 / pomerolrestaurant.com / Open daily

I could say that summer is my favorite season to grab a late-night dinner on Pomerol's sun-drenched back patio, since chilled tomato soup followed by a dozen oysters is not a bad way to close out a busy day. Then again, when the leaves start to do their autumnal thing and a brisk, chilly breeze starts to seep into my bones, I also make my way to the confines here. Their slow-grilled beef short ribs with potatoes two ways (pommes purée and goose fat spuds) will surely hold me over until warmer days prevail. In short, there's never a bad time to visit – you'll always leave satisfied.

RECYCLED CYCLES

New and used bike shop

1109 North 35th Street (near Woodland Park Avenue North)
+1 206 397 4286 / recycledcycles.com / Open daily

Growing up a flatlander, I rode my bike everywhere – even into adulthood.
I would hop on my gorgeous vintage Schwinn coaster and pedal off to
work or to the farmers market, as the bike's basket was just the right size
to carry all of the produce. Soon after I moved to Seattle (famous for its
seven hills), it became clear that coasting about was no longer an option
and that I'd need to upgrade my wheels. It was Recycled Cycles to the
rescue. They are quick with advice and have a large stock of both brand-
new and pre-loved bikes that will make anyone's trek up these hills a little
easier. Plus, they have some pretty awesome coasters for the flatlander in

REVEL

Comfort food from Korea

403 North 36th Street (near Francis Avenue North)
+1 206 547 2040 / revelseattle.com / Open daily

One of the most impressive pantries that I've come across – filled with canned and pickled treats – belongs to Rachel Yang and Seif Chirchi of Revel. Luckily for us, the tasty accoutrements seem to accompany almost everything in this Korean-inspired hot spot. From the pork, collard greens and kimchi dumplings to the Dungeness crab noodles, the fare here pops with flavor. It's been said that if you don't like kimchi, you've never been to Revel. What's more, they're not afraid to share their secrets. Join them for one of their cooking classes to learn how the magic happens.

SUSHI KAPPO TAMURA

Locally sourced dishes

2968 Eastlake Avenue East (near East Allison Street)
+1 206 547 0937 / sushikappotamura.com / Open daily

Rooftop gardens are not usually what I picture when someone mentions sushi. However, bring up Sushi Kappo Tamura and what instantly comes to mind is chef and owner Taichi Kitamura's first shiso harvest being clipped from the plant beds atop the building. Local, sustainable ingredients are not exclusive to this bounty of greens. Sushi Kappo Tamura delivers absolute gems from its open kitchen, serving fish from the waters of Washington, Alaska and British Columbia. This enticing combination of Northwest-sourced land and sea — like the mustard greens with Washington albacore tuna, the Puget Sound chum salmon roe and the Neah Bay black cod, avocado and cucumber roll — are undeniable, as is that rare bottle of sake you'll find on the menu.

TEN22HOME

Mod furnishings

4258 Fremont Avenue North (at North 43rd Street)
+1 206 457 5728 / ten22home.com / Open Thursday through Sunday

Stepping into Ten22home is like walking into an episode of *Mad Men* –
without the cigarette smoke. Although Don Draper may no longer grace our
small screens weekly, it's clear that mid-century style will always be prime-
time ready. For the past decade, shoppers could only find Justin Ferguson's
curation of furniture and décor for sale online, but nowadays, he's making
many homeowners around the Pacific Northwest happy with his intimate
showroom of exemplary finds – stylings from the likes of Arne Jacobsen,
Milo Baughman, George Nelson and other iconic designers. TV period
dramas come and go, but pieces of this pedigree are timeless.

UNEEDA BURGER

Gourmet hamburgers

4302 Fremont Avenue North (near North 43rd Street)
+1 206 547 2600 / uneedaburger.com / Open daily

Remember that childhood song, "I scream, you scream, we all scream for ice cream"? Well, I've made a slight modification, which seems to be more in line with my adult sensibilities: "I need, you need, we all need a burger!" Really, who doesn't want a succulent patty, whose juices you can imagine dripping down your chin at a mere glance? Seems the folks at Uneeda Burger are finely attuned to our cravings. Top off that locally sourced beef, lamb or chicken with some tasty additions – think tempura lemons, roasted chili relish or truffle shoestring potatoes – and you've got yourself a real winner.

WESTWARD

A meal with a view

2501 North Northlake Way (near North 36th Street)
+1 206 552 8215 / westwardseattle.com / Open daily

"Land ahoy!" seems like the appropriate exclamation for Westward —
especially if you arrive via Lake Union. If you're coming in with the tide,
park your boat at their dock, or pull your kayak up on the beach of the
joint's expansive frontage that sports a stunning vista looking across the
water to the city's ever-growing skyline. I usually arrive by car, but still
enjoy the sights — and some grilled octopus — in one of their Adirondack
chairs near the fire pit. Inside, the glow from Westward's wood-fired oven
cannot be ignored as it readies a delicately roasted rainbow trout and
other pleasures of the sea. You won't want to abandon this ship
anytime soon.

what's brewin'

Coffee counter culture

ANALOG COFFEE
235 Summit Avenue East (at East Thomas Street;
Capitol Hill), no phone, analogcoffee.com, open daily

ELM COFFEE ROASTERS
240 2nd Avenue South #103 (near South Main Street;
Pioneer Square), +1 206 445 7808
elmcoffeeroasters.com, open daily

GENERAL PORPOISE
1020 East Union Street (near 10th Avenue;
Capitol Hill), +1 206 900 8770, gpdoughnuts.com
open daily

MILSTEAD & CO.
900 North 34th Street (near Aurora Avenue North;
Fremont), +1 206 659 4814, milsteadandco.com
open daily

SLATE COFFE
5413 6th Avenue Northwest (near Northwest Market
Street; Ballard), no phone, slatecoffee.com
open daily

Seattle may be known as the home of Starbucks, but scratch the surface ever so slightly and you'll discover that some of the most superlative coffee in the country is being roasted and brewed across this city.

The folks at **Analog Coffee** know how much Seattleites like their craft beer, so they took caffeine to the next logical step – kegged and on draft – which means you can fill your growler with cold brew. They also pour some pretty fine cups sourced from local roasters in this chill Capitol Hill hang.

Elm Coffee Roasters scours the world for the choicest beans and brings them home. You won't find cloying blends here: Elm prides itself on serving up the tastiest light roast around. My pick is the Kenya Gathaithi AA – full-bodied, with a hint of ripe blackberry – for a truly delectable start to the day.

General Porpoise may be known for its filled doughnuts (don't skip the rhubarb and Meyer lemon confection), but you would be well advised to take the time to appreciate the joe being served up alongside the tasty, seasonal treats. Roasts from the likes of De Lâ Paz in San Francisco and Toby's Estate in Brooklyn can be enjoyed as a traditional drip, espresso or pour-over.

Tired of the attitude that comes with a lot of coffee shops? Then make a beeline to **Milstead & Co**. in Fremont, where knowledgeable and friendly baristas await, happy to pour you a masterfully brewed java from beloved roasters like Intelligentsia, Stumptown and Coava.

Having a tough time deciding? Then head over to the ever-welcoming **Slate Coffee Roasters** in Ballard and order their tasting flight. Get to know the neighborhood from the regulars and order like one, too, with the popular deconstructed espresso + milk: a three-glass sampler consisting of one glass of espresso, one glass of milk and the last glass with a latte – yes, that does add up to two lattes.

ballard

Ballard has some pretty serious ties to the
Scandinavian seafaring community. Those roots
are on full display during the annual parade that
celebrates Norwegian Constitution Day and at the
Ballard SeafoodFest (lutefisk, anyone?). Even the
holiday season has Scandinavian flair: Santa arrives
to this hood by water in a Norwegian fishing boat
for the Christmas festival. The enclave has quickly
transformed over the last few years though; with an
influx of young tech workers moving in, apartment
buildings have started to dot the skyline that once
primarily consisted of single-family homes. Fortunately,
Ballard Avenue still maintains its link to the past as
many of the watering holes, dining establishments and
shops on this stretch have claimed their homes in the
historic buildings from the early 1900s.

NORTH WEST 77TH ST

NORTH WEST 75TH ST

3

NORTH WEST 70TH ST

9

NORTH WEST 67TH ST

NORTH WEST 65TH ST

1 Bop Street Records
2 Brimmer & Heeltap (off map)
3 Cafe Munir (off map)
4 Card Kingdom
5 Curtis Steiner
6 Lucky Dry Goods
7 Prism
8 Staple & Fancy
9 The Pantry

1

NORTH WEST MARKET ST

D D Line Transfer Point

NORTH WEST 54TH ST

6

5

7

2

4

8

NORTH WEST 56TH ST

BOP STREET RECORDS

Tunes for everyone

2220 Northwest Market Street (near Ballard Avenue Northwest)
+1 206 297 2232 / bopstreetrecords.com / Closed Monday

When digital music first hit the scene, there was a long line of prognosticators ready to declare the death of the LP. Thankfully, their foreshadowing was all kinds of wrong because vinyl is back with a vengeance. You don't have to tell that to Bop Street Records. For them, turntables never fell out of fashion, and this has been one of the preeminent places to get your record fix, regardless of musical taste, for the past 30 years. Stop by on any given night and you'll come across hard-core fans flipping through thousands of albums. Long live cover art, and long live Bop Street Records.

BRIMMER & HEELTAP

Hidden treasure of a gastropub

425 Northwest Market Street (near 6th Avenue Northwest)
+1 206 420 2534 / brimmerandheeltap.com / Closed Tuesday

With the bevy of new residents calling Ballard home, the dining and nightlife scenes have exploded. The energy is fantastic, but if I need a respite from the hustle and bustle, I head a few blocks east to the appealing and casual Brimmer & Heeltap. Tucked steadfast on an unassuming corner, it serves up nourishment for the neighborhood's soul with its locally inspired fare, like steak tartare with daikon, nori (seaweed) rice crackers, and grilled asparagus with Dungeness crab, Aleppo pepper and buttermilk yuzu vinaigrette. The whitewashed interior and exposed beams of this place seem to glow from within – or perhaps it's the light bouncing off the copper and zinc from their floor made of pennies.

CAFE MUNIR

Lebanese eats

2408 Northwest 80th Street (near 24th Avenue Northwest) / +1 206 783 4190
cafemunir.blogspot.com / Closed Monday

In Lebanon, there's a long-standing tradition of a large family meal served weekly that centers around multiple plates of mezze, as people eat, drink and have the occasional argument. Sounds like a couple of my family gatherings – minus the mezze. In Seattle, Cafe Munir hosts this type of dinner every night: it's the place where friends, neighbors and family can get together to relax, restore and share in some authentic Middle Eastern fare. The café succeeds as one of the most charming restaurants around, and it has people coming from all over the city to get a little taste of Lebanon in Loyal Heights. Be sure to order the muhammara (red pepper and chili) kafta, batinjan Josephine (labne with roasted onion, eggplant, zucchini and tomatoes), and don't skip the nut and date ma'amoul (shortbread) for dessert.

CARD KINGDOM

A gamer's paradise

5105 Leary Avenue Northwest (near Northwest Dock Place)
+1 206 523 2273 / cardkingdom.com / Open daily

Remember those kids in high school who would disappear to their basements on the weekends to play Dungeons & Dragons throughout the night? Well, many of those D&D players are now leaders of our free world. If you want to see who the next batch of movers and shakers will be, head down to Card Kingdom. Whether you're a tyke, teenager or adult, this tabletop gaming shop will no doubt have whatever it is that you and your friends are dying to play. And if you can't wait to start, take your game to Café Mox, which is located in the same space – grab a beverage and some sustenance, then start dominating.

CURTIS STEINER

Victorian emporium

5349 Ballard Avenue Northwest (near 22nd Avenue Northwest)
+1 206 297 7116 / curtissteiner.com / Closed Monday and Tuesday

When I'm shopping, there are usually certain sections I tend to quickly
glance over, registering the items but knowing my true interests lie
elsewhere. Not so at Curtis Steiner. There are no cursory glances here.
Every single piece of jewelry, sculpture and even the fixtures are chosen
and cleverly displayed by Curtis himself. Simply looking through his highly
sought-after, handmade greeting cards could take up an entire afternoon
– time well spent, I might add. Like a museum that holds so many gems
it demands repeat visits, Curtis's curated vision of turn-of-the-century
elegance and design will beckon you back more than once.

LUCKY DRY GOODS

Secondhand clothing trove

5424 Ballard Avenue Northwest (near Northwest Market Street)
+1 206 789 8191 / luckyvintageseattle.com / Open daily

"Sooner or later, everything old is new again". Attribute that quote to whomever you like – all I know is that when I'm looking for an outfit so flawless it would have been worthy of '20s "It girl" Clara Bow, I head straight to Lucky Dry Goods. Carefully stocked, this shop has some of the top retro buyers on staff, making sure the pre-loved clothes you drape on your back, no matter what decade they shined, are appropriately of the moment. Grab a sheath dress from the '50s, a brightly patterned men's shirt or a pair of '70s high-waisted jeans and hit the town – these threads come ready to wear.

PRISM

Thoughtfully chosen wearables and home goods

5208 Ballard Avenue Northwest (near 20th Avenue Northwest)
+1 206 402 4706 / templeofcairo.com/prism / Open daily

It doesn't matter how many times I walk past the windows of Prism,
I always find myself compelled to pop in and check out the clever items
they've assembled for the soon-to-be gifts for my friends, family and,
let's be honest, myself. The sun always seems to cooperate, drenching
everything through their front windows in light. The last time I stopped by,
I spied a stylishly casual chambray linen coat, a handsome solar-powered
watch and a mushroom knife perfect for foraging chanterelles in locations
that are to ever remain a secret. See? Plenty of gifts for everyone.

STAPLE & FANCY

Rustic food in a historic building

4739 Ballard Avenue Northwest (near Northwest 48th Street)
+1 206 789 1200 / ethanstowellrestaurants.com / Open daily

With Staple & Fancy, chef Ethan Stowell has been holding down the
south end of Ballard Avenue since 2010. It's still undeniably buzzy,
but given most of Ballard's nightlife (and noise) tends to gravitate toward
the north end, this Italian-inspired eatery is a fantastic place to sit down
and thoroughly enjoy an evening's meal. Exposed brick walls featuring old,
hand-painted murals and original wood plank floors in this former marine
supply building only add to the experience. You can order à la carte – the
wood-grilled whole fish coming out of the open kitchen is amazing – but if
you want the full experience, the chef's choice tasting menu is the way to go.

THE PANTRY

Pint-sized cooking school

1417 Northwest 70th Street (near Alonzo Avenue Northwest)
+1 206 436 1064 / thepantryseattle.com / Open daily

I'm all about community, so when The Pantry dubbed itself a communal
kitchen, I was immediately all in. Sign up online for one of the many classes
here and you'll be joining like-minded souls learning to cure your own
meats, create a masterfully blistered pizza pie, mix a mean cocktail, make a
Montreal-style bagel or partake in just about any other experience you can
think of that relates to food. It's a hands-on, immersive affair where you
can't help but meet neighbors and make new friends while breaking bread.
The Pantry should be a standard in everyone's life.

remarkable microbrews

Grab your growler

These days it almost doesn't matter which craft brewery you stop by, you're guaranteed to find three things: adorable dogs, parents with kids in tow and some of the premier seasonal ales and house pours in the Pacific Northwest.

You'll definitely want to drop in at **Holy Mountain Brewing**, an understated taproom that has captured the hearts of many in this region. It's the ultimate spot to chill over some incredible pints, like Covenant, a barrel-fermented saison. They also crank out excellent special release bottles – like the dark, oaky Tower of Babel farmhouse ale – every couple of months.

At **Optimism Brewing Co.**, they help make your selection that much easier to choose by providing thirst-inducing photos of each beer and non-jargon-y flavor descriptions. For example, the brewer explains their popular One label as tasting of sweet toffee, lingering caramel, malt and a well-balanced hop flavor. Sounds perfect.

The tasting room at **Populuxe Brewing** is a tad snug, but step outside to the courtyard and see your beer-drinking world expand. On sunny days, sit at the picnic tables and sip on a Jet City IPA while waiting your turn for the next round of cornhole. If the forecast calls for rain, take shelter by the covered fire pit and enjoy the slightly sweet and fruity Precipitation Porter.

HOLY MOUNTAIN BREWING
1421 Elliott Avenue West (near West Galer Street;
Queen Anne), no phone, holymountainbrewing.com
open daily

OPTIMISM BREWING CO.
1158 Broadway (at East Union Street; Capitol Hill)
+1 206 651 5429, optimismbrewing.com
closed Monday

POPULUXE BREWING
826B Northwest 49th Street (near 9th
Avenue Northwest; Ballard), +1 206 706 3400
populuxebrewing.com, open Thursday through Sunday

REUBEN'S BREWS
5010 14th Avenue Northwest (near Northwest 51st
Street; Ballard), +1 206 784 2859, reubensbrews.com
open daily

STOUP BREWING
1108 Northwest 52nd Street (near 11th Avenue
Northwest; Ballard), +1 206 457 5524
stoupbrewing.com, open daily

You don't have to travel too far from Populuxe to find your next hangout.
Reuben's Brew is three blocks away and has nearly two dozen beers available
at any given time. That means you'll have no excuse not finding just the right
draft, like their award-winning, bitter Imperial IPA.

Next, swing by **Stoup Brewing** and join the fun-loving crowd that seems to be
ever-present seven days a week. There's a reason for this: Stoup is methodical
in its brewing technique and consistently has appealing creations on tap.
How else can you explain the spicy saison, Hoppy Farmhouse?

HOLY MOUNTAIN BREWING

belltown and queen anne

"Leafy" and "green" are the two adjectives most often attributed to Queen Anne. That's because it's chock full of outdoor spaces – 25 in all. The most heavily trafficked is Kerry Park; at a little over 1.25 acres, it may be small but the view is huge, with sweeping vistas overlooking the Space Needle and Mount Rainier in the distance. Mainly residential, the area's retail core is concentrated up on top of the hill that is Queen Anne Avenue. Head back down, just south of Lower Queen Anne (or Uptown, as it's recently been dubbed), and you'll be in the very walkable Belltown. This enclave is quiet during the morning, but comes alive midday and stays hopping until late into the night. Known for its wide mix of eateries, bars and nightclubs, Belltown seems to be constantly abuzz, making this hot spot less residential and more of a destination.

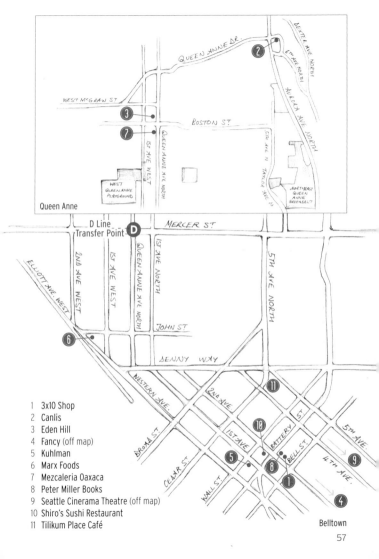

Queen Anne

D Line
Transfer Point

1 3x10 Shop
2 Canlis
3 Eden Hill
4 Fancy (off map)
5 Kuhlman
6 Marx Foods
7 Mezcaleria Oaxaca
8 Peter Miller Books
9 Seattle Cinerama Theatre (off map)
10 Shiro's Sushi Restaurant
11 Tilikum Place Café

Belltown

57

3X10 SHOP

Inspired housewares

2324 2nd Avenue (near Battery Street) / +1 206 256 0809
suyamapetersondeguchi.com / Closed Saturday and Sunday

Architects Suyama, Peterson and Deguchi have a goal of "creating spaces that evoke a quiet, emotional response". Well, I think they nailed it with their 3x10 Shop, located just inside the front door of their architecture studio. It's an intimate space filled with beautifully designed and consciously selected décor from this venerable trio. Inch your way through the collection to find custom-fabricated furniture and accessories made with attention to natural materials that would warm any dwelling. Interspersed throughout are equally striking handcrafted works by local artisans, intriguing found objects and stunning coffee table books.

CANLIS

Iconic fine dining with a view

2576 Aurora Avenue North (near 6th Avenue North)
+1 206 283 3313 / canlis.com / Closed Sunday

Ask any Seattleite where to go for a celebratory meal and they'll point you in the direction of Canlis. Perched high over Lake Union, you know you're in for a special night as you watch the sun set over the Cascade Mountains. Revel in the multi-course meals — including Copper River King salmon, black cod, Dungeness crab and dry-aged duck — and don't miss the famous Canlis salad, prepared tableside, straight from their great-grandmother's recipe. It's similar to a classic Caesar, but has mint and oregano mixed in for pops of brightness. You shouldn't let a yearly milestone be the driving factor for your visit; dining at Canlis is a celebration all unto itself, any day of the year.

EDEN HILL

Imaginative fare in a warm environment

2209 Queen Anne Avenue North (near West Boston Street)
+1 206 708 6836 / edenhillrestaurant.com / Closed Monday

There was a time when the main drag of upper Queen Anne had a welcoming neighborhood feel. Over the years (and many condo developments later), some of that quaintness has been lost. Fortunately, chef Maximillian Petty moved back to Seattle after working in upscale dining establishments across the US, opened Eden Hill and brought with him some of the close-knit community vibe that had seemed to disappear — not to mention his progressive New American cuisine. His 24-seat restaurant is a charmer that brings neighbors together to dine over inventive creations, like the crispy pig head "candybar" and the blueback sockeye with sea bean chimichurri and pork skin chicharron. Welcome back, chef.

FANCY

Jewelry custom made for you

1914 2nd Avenue (near Stewart Street) / +1 206 956 2945
heyfancy.com / Closed Sunday and Monday

Calling all newly engaged: it's time to start making decisions – wedding location, guest list, the honeymoon. One of the biggest decisions to make is choosing the rings you'll exchange at the altar. This is where Fancy comes in. Co-owner Sally Brock has built a reputation matching lovestruck couples with magnificently designed, unique wedding bands. Granted, you don't need to have a trip planned down the aisle to get in on the action. Fancy offers up a whole range of customizable jewelry as well as items for the home, designed and crafted by leading metalsmiths and artists from around the country. You can't get much fancier than that.

KUHLMAN

Bespoke creations

2419 1st Avenue (near Wall Street) / +1 206 441 1999
kuhlmanseattle.com / Open daily

The first thing I usually notice when walking into Kuhlman is the large neon "K" on the back wall. That said, my focus quickly adjusts below to the bolts of well-appointed fabric that will soon become the bones for one lucky person's tailor-made suit. The boutique's namesake, Scott Kuhlman, is the man behind the threads, and he has been responsible for some of the sharpest-dressed people in Seattle for nearly two decades. It's not only his handmade suits people seek out, though. Kuhlman carries heritage brands like Lacoste and Ben Sherman right alongside the up-and-comers, keeping us all on trend.

MARX FOODS

Specialty grocer

144 Western Avenue West (near West John Street) / +1 206 447 1818
marxfoods.com / Closed Saturday and Sunday

Don't let the dehydrated black ants sealed in a 10-gram can throw you off. They're actually pretty tasty, plus they pack a good protein punch. It's unusual items like this, along with the fresh produce, seafood and a wide array of exotic meats, that makes home cooks looking for the same ingredients being used by some of the top chefs around the country head to Marx Foods. Whether you have a hankering for some alligator Andouille sausage or magret duck breasts, this place can hook you up. Their assortment of pantry goods is also a delight and features many must-haves that you didn't know were must-haves until you tried them, like my fave, cherry rosehip hibiscus jam.

MEZCALERIA OAXACA

Fresh Oaxacan fare

2123 Queen Anne Avenue North (near West Boston Street)
+1 206 216 4446 / mezcaleriaoaxaca.com / Closed Sunday

I highly suggest visiting the Mexican state of Oaxaca, especially if you can make it around Dia de los Muertos. Oaxaca City comes alive with endless celebrations punctuated with the vibrant color of marigolds scattered throughout. Can't make the trip? Dining at Mezcaleria Oaxaca is the next best thing. You'll instantly be transported to Mexico with this eatery's energy, black-and-white photos from the homeland, ofrendas (altars) and, of course, the food. The mole is served up rich and sweet. The slow-roasted goat literally falls apart. As for the smoky spirit of Oaxaca? It's found in the mezcal tasting flight.

PETER MILLER BOOKS

Endless inspiration

2326 2nd Avenue (near Battery Street) / +1 206 441 4114
petermiller.com / Closed Sunday

Historically, Seattle may not always be inextricably linked to being
en vogue, but for more than 35 years, Peter Miller Books in Belltown has
been the city's harbinger of design. I could browse these bookshelves for
days, finding the latest and greatest on architecture, landscape, urban
planning and graphics. The aesthetics here aren't just discovered on the
page, but are found in every corner of this shop. If you have a penchant for
high-end pens and pencils, Peter has handpicked the ultimate options,
and the Le Corbusier stencil set is tough to resist. Timeless décor, like an
littala Aalto vase, are also available to admire – and take home.

SEATTLE CINERAMA THEATRE

Nostalgic moviegoing

2100 4th Avenue (at Lenora Street) / +1 206 448 6680
cinerama.com / Open daily

I'm a huge fan of watching movies, and even though it's been almost
20 years since the day I heard homegrown hero Paul Allen was stepping
in with a multimillion-dollar renovation to save the historic Cinerama,
I'm still more than thrilled that he did. Today, this cinema is Seattle's prime
picturehouse, and boasts one of the biggest screens in the city – some films
are even shown in 70mm. The lobby is wonderfully '60s retro and sci-fi fans
can find original costumes from *Star Wars* and *Blade Runner* on display.
There's also a concession stand with a liquor license: pass the chocolate
popcorn and craft cider, please.

SHIRO'S SUSHI RESTAURANT

Succulent rolls and sashimi

2401 2nd Avenue (near Battery Street) / +1 206 443 9844
shiros.com / Open daily

My preferred seat at Shiro's is at the coveted sushi bar, right up close to the action (I highly recommend it). Lines start to form at least 30 minutes before they open at 5:30pm, so show up early if you hope to get in for the first wave of service. It's basically been this way since 1994, when the original master sushi chef, Shiro Kashiba, opened for business. He recently handed his kitchen over with much care to sushi chef Jun Takai and his adroit team, who have taken up the mantle, artfully slicing through local and seasonal seafood like geoduck and Pacific albacore tuna night after night.

TILIKUM PLACE CAFÉ

Cozy eatery

407 Cedar Street (near 4th Avenue) / +1 206 282 4830
tilikumplacecafe.com / Open daily

A tree-lined lane dotted with appealing bistros seems like it would be
easy to find. But quaint escapes from the daily routine of Seattle are few
and far between – unless you know to turn off 4th Avenue onto the tiny,
verdant street that is home to Tilikum. This European-inspired darling
sits in the shadow of the Space Needle – one of the busiest destinations
in the city. There may be thousands of people a stone's throw away, but
when you're here, unwinding over pan-seared chicken and a glass of wine,
you'll feel a million miles from it all.

let bivalves be bivalves

Where to slurp oysters

LITTLE GULL GROCERY
2501 North Northlake Way (near North 37th Street;
Eastlake), +1 206 552 8215, westwardseattle.com
open daily

SALTED SEA
4915 Rainier Avenue South (near South Hudson Street;
Columbia City), +1 206 858 6328
saltedseaseattle.com, open daily

TAYLOR SHELLFISH
1521 Melrose Avenue (near Pine Street; Capitol Hill)
+1 206 501 4321, taylorshellfishfarms.com
open daily

THE BROOKLYN SEAFOOD,
STEAK & OYSTER HOUSE
1212 2nd Avenue (at University Street; Downtown)
+1 206 224 7000, thebrooklyn.com
open daily

THE WALRUS AND THE CARPENTER
4743 Ballard Avenue Northwest (near Northwest
48th Street; Ballard), +1 206 395 9227
thewalrusbar.com, open daily

Olympias, Kumamotos, Pacifics, Virginicas – just to name a few. One could argue that Washington State has the market cornered when it comes to superb oysters. Then again, who has time to argue when there are half shells to be devoured?

A Seattle mainstay, **The Brooklyn Seafood, Steak & Oyster House** has been shucking for the Downtown crowd for more than 25 years. Get the baker's dozen and let the chef choose 13 beauties from their daily selection, or take your pick based on geography – the menu includes locations hailing from up and down the Pacific coast.

So not "downtown," **Little Gull Grocery** is a laid-back joint off Lake Union where you can belly up to the bar and order freshly shucked, locally harvested shellfish along with an ice-cold beer. After you've downed your fair share of the many Pacific varieties on hand, check out the Gull's pantry for a little grab-and-go of beverages, charcuterie and other fixings, for whatever adventures may ensue.

When the clock hits the happiest of hours, stop by **Salted Sea** in Columbia City for $1 oysters. It's a crazy-good deal, especially since it includes the Minter Sweet Selects, some of the tastiest gems from the Pacific Northwest. Don't fret if you miss the 3pm to 5pm window as the fresh assortment at the raw bar will keep you plenty happy.

The granddaddy of oyster farmers, **Taylor Shellfish** has been in the biz since the 1890s. No need to go to one of their farms to enjoy their hard work, though. Stop by their shop and get some of the cleanest shucked mollusks you'll ever throw back. Kusshi, Shigoku, Fat Bastard – you name 'em, they've got 'em.

Drop in at **The Walrus and the Carpenter** for some briny wonders that are almost as legendary as the tale of the same name penned by Lewis Carroll. You'll find yourself salivating at the mere sight of these suckers on display the minute you walk in the door. All Washington State-sourced, the dozen you order will likely turn into two.

downtown

It may not seem like it now, but Downtown was once sleepy – save for a few strip clubs and pawn shops. Today, headlines scream, "Downtown Seattle's Building Frenzy: 65 Projects Now in Construction". Given that about two-thirds of those projects are residential, I think it's safe to say that Downtown is sleepy no more (not to mention free of strip clubs and pawn shops). Noteworthy restaurants are opening up at breakneck speed, all vying to capture the hearts and stomachs of office workers and residents, and art museums, performance halls and nightclubs are also part of the burgeoning mix. Homeowners once content to live in a quiet community are finding themselves charmed with all of this new buzz and are gearing up to be in the heart of the city. Downtown will no longer be denied.

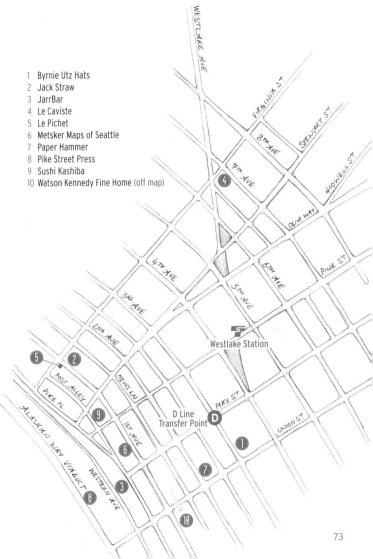

1 Byrnie Utz Hats
2 Jack Straw
3 JarrBar
4 Le Caviste
5 Le Pichet
6 Metsker Maps of Seattle
7 Paper Hammer
8 Pike Street Press
9 Sushi Kashiba
10 Watson Kennedy Fine Home (off map)

Westlake Station

D Line
Transfer Point

BYRNIE UTZ HATS

High tops

310 Union Street (near 3rd Avenue) / +1 206 623 0233
byrnieutz.com / Open daily

You can never have too much headwear, right? At least that's what I tell
myself every time I get a new Kangol cap at Byrnie Utz. After more than
80 years in the same location, stepping into this hattery is like taking a
trip back in time. Chapeaus of legendary pedigree, like Stetson, Biltmore
and Stefeno, sit side by side. Myriad styles reach from floor to ceiling,
waiting to be tried on and expertly fitted by the genial shopkeepers.
You know that genuine Montecristi Panama lid you've always wanted?
It's in stock here. All of your dapper desires are within reach at Byrnie Utz.

JACK STRAW

Chic men's and women's garb

1930 1st Avenue (near Virginia Street) / +1 206 462 6236
jstraw.com / Open daily

You never know from where inspiration is going to strike. It could be a deep meditative state that sows the seeds of greatness, or a muse that leads to enlightenment. But... the Grateful Dead? There's no denying that Jack Straw is both a song penned by the hippie group and a truly inspired store. (The tune is a favorite of the owner.) The latest collections from top designers, such as Barena Vinezia, Engineered Garments, Issey Miyake and Nooy are represented here. In fact, fashion for ladies and gents has never looked more hip than in these understated digs. This ultra-stylish house of design might be anathema to the Dead's fashion sensibility, but count me in as forever grateful.

JARRBAR

Simply delicious

Pike Place Market, 1432 Western Avenue (near Pike Street Hillclimb)
+1 206 209 2239 / jarrbar.com / Open daily

The beauty of JarrBar is in the restraint of their plating. Most everything you need comes to your table in jars and tins stacked atop plates. There are jars of house pickles and smoked king salmon rillettes; tins of anchovies, mussels and octopi; and plates of cured Spanish meats and jamón ibérico. Bottles of wine hail from Iberia and the libations come from the small, lively bar where patrons often order up a potent mix of Nuestra Soledad mezcal with lime and jalapeño. Grab a communal table with some friends or say hello to your fellow tablemates – the welcoming vibe is intoxicating.

LE CAVISTE

Calling all Francophiles and oenophiles

1919 7th Avenue (near Virginia Street) / +1 206 728 2657
lecavisteseattle.com / Closed Sunday

When you want an exceptional bottle of vino, your best bet is to go
to a sommelier who knows their way around a French cellar. In this city,
I would advise that you put your money on David Butler and his *bar à vin*,
Le Caviste. Ducking into this alluring spot is like being transported to a
bistro in Paris. Over two dozen vintages offered by the glass are noted on
the chalkboard, which just about matches the number of seats in this cozy
room. If for some reason you cannot live on wine alone, the charcuterie,
fromage and poisson en papillote (baked fish) coming out of the tiny
kitchen are key ingredients to *la bonne vie*.

LE PICHET

Classically French

Pike Place Market, 1933 1st Avenue (near Virginia Street)
+1 206 256 1499 / lepichetseattle.com / Open daily

You're going to have to settle in at your table and wait for about an hour if you order the *poulet roti* at Le Pichet. It may not sound like time well spent, but let me tell you, it is. Roasted to order, this whole chicken comes to the table with flageolet beans, turnips, carrots and nettle-walnut pistou. The scene at Le Pichet is as outstanding as the dishes they serve – it's a supreme place to begin your day with a filling brunch or end your evening with a luxurious meal. If you happen to be around on Bastille Day, Le Pichet has been known to bust out live music and serve Parisian street food well into the evening.

METSKER MAPS OF SEATTLE

Never feel lost

Pike Place Market, 1511 1st Avenue (near Pike Street)
+1 206 623 8747 / metskers.com / Open daily

I love running across people visiting Seattle. Their excitement for discovering a new place is contagious as they search out new sights, sounds and tastes. Besides the big smiles on their faces, visitors can usually be spotted clutching the guide map that the Convention & Visitors Bureau hands out by the thousands. For me, I prefer to get my bearings straight before I arrive at my destination, via a stop at Metsker Maps. They have cartographs of different shapes and sizes, covering all corners of this big blue marble. They even have maps for a trip into outer space! Go big or go home, right?

PAPER HAMMER

Pulpy gifts

1400 2nd Avenue (at Union Street) / +1 206 682 3820
paper-hammer.com / Closed Sunday

What is it about an invitation, book, or work of art that has been created with a 100-year-old press? Perhaps it's the sense of nostalgia you get from the rough-edged impressions on the page. Or maybe it's the direct connection to the old-school craftsmanship when you run your fingers across the print. Either way, if you're a design and typeface freak, you'll go gaga for Paper Hammer. Hot off the presses come plenty of striking designs that have been committed to card stock. So what are you waiting for, Helvetica lovers? Seems like Paper Hammer is just your type.

PIKE STREET PRESS

Custom letterpress shop and gallery

1510 Alaskan Way (near Pike Street Hillclimb) / +1 206 971 0120
pikestreetpress.com / Open daily

To pinpoint when my love affair with the printed word began, I have to go all the way back to a grade-school field trip to my hometown's local newspaper. Learning about the origins of print and watching thousands of sheets of paper glide across the ink-stained plate was intoxicating. Looking to rekindle your love with the art of printing? Pike Street Press will definitely fan the flame. Personalized invitations, gift cards, posters and other printed matter are lovingly rolled out on a big ol' Heidelberg press. But enough of that already – you had me at Gutenberg.

SUSHI KASHIBA

Skillfully prepared raw eats

86 Pine Street, Suite #1 (near Post Alley) / +1 206 441 8844
sushikashiba.com / Open daily

Several years ago, I was on a ferry to Bainbridge Island with sushi chef
and author Shiro Kashiba, where he was surrounded by passengers as he
read from his book. It was classic Shiro – a humble reading from a revered
cuisinier who trained in Tokyo with heralded chef Jiro Ono in the '60s.
His latest venture, Sushi Kashiba, is also classic Shiro. On almost any
night, you can find him behind the counter delighting and guiding his
patrons through the flavors and textures of the nigiri he respectfully
prepares with his light touch. His food is complex, yet simple – the sign
of a true master.

WATSON KENNEDY FINE HOME

Purveyor of magnificent goods

1022 1st Avenue (near Spring Street) / +1 206 652 8350
watsonkennedy.com / Open daily

When I was in Madrid, a trip down El Rastro (where a large, open-air flea market takes place) would leave me uncharacteristically short on focus; each corner I turned would propel me toward an amazing assortment of treasures in every shop I passed. It's the same at Watson Kennedy, where the counters and shelves are filled with gifts, jewelry, art and nearly anything else one could imagine. I showed considerable restraint and left Spain with a single antique key, but here, I tend to leave with much more.

pioneer square

sodo

Considered Seattle's first downtown neighborhood, Pioneer Square has mellowed since the time it was home to one of the original skid rows. Even so, it still has a raucous feel, which is perhaps why it's been enjoying a renaissance of late. Found south of Downtown, this community is attracting businesses ranging from tech start-ups to established companies. They're all laying claim to spacious office digs in historic buildings, hoping to pull in savvy employees and beat the development craze. Not everything here is gentrifying, though: the brick-paved Occidental Square Park is often a hub of residential activity, and 1st Avenue is still lined with many of the old-timey taverns that gave this area its early reputation – these watering holes are just the ticket before heading to a ball game in one of the two nearby stadiums in SoDo.

1 E. Smith Mercantile
2 Il Corvo Pasta
3 Manu's Bodega
4 Pier 50 Water Taxi to Marination Ma Kai (off map)
5 Smith Tower
6 The London Plane
7 Velouria
8 Westland Distillery (off map)

E. SMITH MERCANTILE

General store for modern living

208 1st Avenue South (near South Washington Street)
+1 206 641 7250 / esmithmercantile.com / Open daily

If you're not sure what you need, you'll definitely know once you step
inside E. Smith Mercantile. The exposed brick walls in this lovely shop
are lined with housewares, clothing, jewelry, foodstuffs for your pantry
and handcrafted apothecary goods. Take your time as you wander through
– the sense of place here encourages it – as there are plenty of discoveries
to be made. Hopefully you'll mosey far enough to find The Back Bar,
a snug, 12-seat space that's wonderful for meeting up with friends or
taking a break from shopping. Like the emporium up front, they concoct
many of their own infusions for the ultimate counterpart to your post-
shopping cocktail.

IL CORVO PASTA

Noodles worth waiting for

217 James Street (near 3rd Avenue) / +1 206 538 0999
ilcorvopasta.com / Closed Saturday and Sunday

Standing in line is not something I enjoy, but when it comes to lunching at Il Corvo, the wait (and there will be one) is well worth it. It's not hard to understand why people are willing to queue: every day, three handmade pastas are posted on Il Corvo's board, signaling what awaits the hungry patrons. Porcini tagliarini, gigli (ruffly, bell-shaped pasta) with ricotta and pesto, and lumache (shell-shaped pasta) with Italian sausage and Tuscan kale are just a few recent rotating creations. With only 36 seats, it can get intimate, but everyone seems to become fast friends with these dishes in front of them.

MANU'S BODEGA

Lively Latin hideaway

100 Prefontaine Place South (near Yesler Way) / +1 206 682 2175
manusbodega.com / Closed Saturday and Sunday

The first time I met Manu Alfau was at a rooftop paella party that was
one for the books. Fitting, really, as I tend to run into him these days over
memorable afternoon meals at his eatery. Carved out on a busy street
that attracts all walks of life, Manu's Bodega is a colorful and cheery lunch
hangout with small wooden tables surrounded by stools, where people
gather over food and music. Bands often play in the small courtyard,
where bright blue tin tables are set out on the deck, creating a marvelous
soundtrack of Latin American tunes for you to enjoy some beef picadillo
empanadas or a Cuban dip sandwich made with slow-roasted pork.
At Manu's, it seems the party never ends.

PIER 50 WATER TAXI TO MARINATION MA KAI

It's about the journey and the destination

801 Alaskan Way (at Yesler Way) / No phone
kingcounty.gov/transportation / Open daily

This is probably the best way ever to arrive to a dining venue. Make your way to Pioneer Square's waterfront, pay the inexpensive fare and board the water taxi. Fifteen minutes later, you'll pull up at the doorstep of Marination Ma Kai in West Seattle. The view of the skyline is a stunner as you cross Elliott Bay, and it continues to unfold once you're casually noshing on some Hawaiian-Korean cuisine on the deck, looking back at the city. After your last kalua pork slider or miso ginger chicken taco, jump back on the boat and take in an amazing sunset on your return.

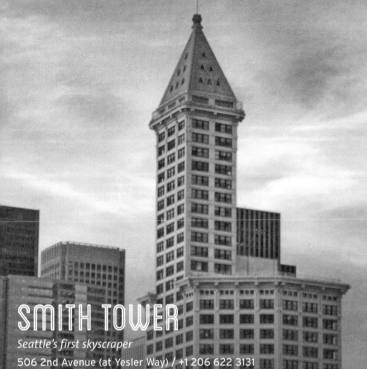

SMITH TOWER

Seattle's first skyscraper

506 2nd Avenue (at Yesler Way) / +1 206 622 3131
smithtower.com / Open daily

Looking at the city skyline today, it's hard to imagine that Smith Tower was once the tallest building west of the Mississippi River. However, hop on the Otis elevator trimmed in copper and brass to be whisked to the 35th floor, and you'll feel like you're sitting on top of the world. It's not hard to imagine what it would be like back in the '20s while you're sipping on a Manhattan in the Tower's speakeasy, Smith Tower Temperance, which harkens back to those unthinkable days of prohibition. Marble interiors, hand-carved ceilings and panoramic views of the cityscape only add to this landmark's allure.

THE LONDON PLANE

For all your senses

300 Occidental Avenue South (near South Main Street) / +1 206 624 1374
thelondonplaneseattle.com / Open daily

The storefront of The London Plane is an excellent calling card – you're immediately drawn in by the colorful bunches of flowers that spill out onto the brick-paved plaza. Once you're inside, you may find it tough to leave. Carefully chosen items, from housewares to art that would make marvelous gifts, line the shelves. The aroma of fresh bread from the on-site bakery will have you making your way to their café, and the seared pork belly coming out of their kitchen will seal the deal. If they had you with the blossoms, their floral arrangement class is a fab way to learn while drinking Champagne and enjoying light bites.

VELOURIA

Sweet frock shop

145 South King Street (near Occidental Avenue South)
+1 206 788 0330 / shopvelouria.com / Open daily

Owners Cat and Chika have gathered some of the choicest pieces from Northwest designers in their lovely boutique. Whether it's the perfect-for-summer Laysan hand-printed linen pants from a Seattle-based atelier or a striped A-line dress that hails from our neighbors to the south in Portland, it's clear independently made clothing has a friend in Velouria — which makes Velouria a friend of mine. Though wares from Pacific Northwest creators are well represented, limited edition dresses, accessories and home goods by indie designers from San Francisco to Brooklyn, and across the pond to London can also be found. Best friends forever.

WESTLAND DISTILLERY

Whiskey whisperers

2931 1st Avenue South, Suite B (near South Hanford Street)
+1 206 767 7250 / westlanddistillery.com / Closed Sunday
and Monday

Forget Scotland. When you're trying to find that quintessential single malt,
you don't have to go very far to get one of the finest in the country. In SoDo,
past the warehouses and stadiums, Westland Distillery has emerged as
a leader among American distillers. I could talk about all of the awards
they've won, but the proof is right there in the barrels made out of trees
felled from nearby forests. Speaking of which, a visit to their expansive
tasting room is a peaty and smoky must; do yourself a favor and don't
skip the 45-minute tour. I can guarantee that you'll leave with at least
one bottle of single malt.

inspiring perspectives

Defying convention

Art from the Northwest School movement was known for its earthy, moody tones. Today, local artists have moved way beyond those mystics, and are creating vibrant, edgy work that reflects a new era for this region. Hit up these museums and galleries to get your eye-full.

For years, Dawna Holloway created art in her Georgetown studio. Now she's showcasing the work of local and international artists, such as Brian Cypher, Carole d'Inverno and Curtis Steiner (see pg 49) at **studio e**. This modern gallery plays host to some of the most relevant art happening in the city today.

Frye Art Museum pushes the envelope a bit more than others. Works and performances that might turn heads in some museums, like *Future Ruins* by Seattle-based video artist and photographer Rodrigo Valenzuela, and *Young Blood*, which explored the artistic relationship between brothers Kahlil Joseph and the late Noah Davis, fit comfortably alongside the pastoral works that Charles and Emma Frye left behind more than 70 years ago.

My most anticipated exhibits, like Ann Hamilton's *the common S E N S E*, are usually found at the **Henry Art Gallery**. It's also home to one of my favorite spots to sneak away for a quick, meditative respite: James Turrell's immersive sculpture, *Skyspace*.

As you glance at the pieces from the international contemporary artists gracing the walls at **Mariane Ibrahim Gallery**, it's likely you won't recognize many of the names: Mustapha Azeroual, Sofie Knijff, Clay Apenouvon, Zohra Opoku. What you will recognize is the amazing work that definitely deserves to be seen by a wider audience. And thanks to Mariane, it is.

FRYE ART MUSEUM
704 Terry Avenue (at Cherry Street; First Hill)
+1 206 622 9250, fryemuseum.org, closed Monday

HENRY ART GALLERY
4100 15th Avenue Northeast (near Northeast Campus Parkway;
University District), +1 206 543 2280, henryart.org
closed Monday and Tuesday

MARIANE IBRAHIM GALLERY
608 2nd Avenue (near James Street; Pioneer Square)
+1 206 467 4927, marianeibrahim.com
closed Sunday and Monday, Tuesday by appointment

PHOTOGRAPHIC CENTER NORTHWEST
900 12th Avenue (at East Marion Street; Squire Park)
+1 206 720 7222, pcnw.org, closed Friday

STUDIO E
609 South Brandon Street (near 6th Avenue South; Georgetown)
+1 206 762 3322, studioegallery.org
open Friday and Saturday, and by appointment

TASHIRO KAPLAN ARTIST LOFTS
115 Prefontaine Place South (near 4th Avenue South;
Pioneer Square), +1 206 223 1160, tklofts.com, closed Monday

Visit **Photographic Center Northwest** and you'll probably catch a faint whiff of film chemicals: classes and workshops that are open to anyone interested are held here. Meanwhile, the front room is always curated with thoughtful exhibits – like *Enduring Freedom* by Eugene Richards, which marked the 15th anniversary of September 11th. One visit here and you'll want to be a lifetime student.

Walk around **Tashiro Kaplan Artist Lofts** and you'll trip across nearly a dozen respected galleries: artists either live in one of the 50 affordable lofts above or create in one of the two dozen studios within. It's a main draw when First Thursday art walks roll around – drop by my picks SOIL and Gallery4Culture, but make sure you see as many as you can, as everything here is worth your time.

international district

Depending on whom you talk to (and their history with the area), you may hear this part of town referred to as Chinatown, Japantown or Little Saigon. Mostly you'll hear it as the International District, or "the ID". Home to the Asian-American community, this hood bustles with activity year round. It's where Seattleites flock for the explosive Lunar New Year celebration and for the colorful Chinese lion and dragon dances during the annual Dragon Fest. In the fall, the night markets draw us in and, of course, we're prone to gather here on weekends for the tastiest dim sum the city has to offer. It doesn't really matter what day of the week, or what time of the day you visit the ID: it's the residents that make it come alive with energy and a true sense of place all year long.

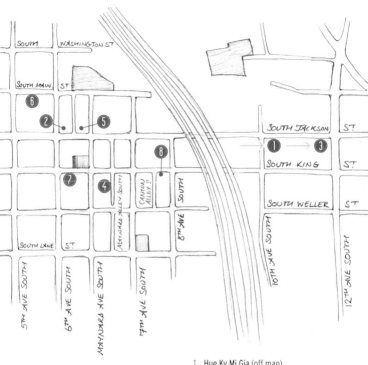

1 Hue Ky Mi Gia (off map)
2 MOMO
3 Northwest Tofu (off map)
4 Seattle Pinball Museum
5 Trichome
6 Tsukushinbo
7 Venus Karaoke
8 Wing Luke Museum of the Asian Pacific
   American Experience

HUE KY MI GIA

Crave-inducing Chinese and Vietnamese cuisine

1207 South Jackson Street, Suite 101 (near 12th Avenue South)
+1 206 568 1268 / huekymigia.com / Closed Tuesday

My partner was never crazy about chicken wings. He just didn't get the
hype. At least, not until our first dinner at Hue Ky Mi Gia. Maybe it was
the butter-crusted glaze, because he finally got ahold of his senses and
relented to some of the most delectable wings in town. As amazing as
they are, they're actually not why everyone comes here. Families flock to
this friendly enclave to slurp up noodles by the bowl-full, like the braised
duck with Chinese herbs and spices. That said, when you go, you should
definitely order the wings — I suggest requesting at least two plates,
since one is never enough.

momo

Peachy attire and accoutrements

600 South Jackson Street (near 6th Avenue South)
+1 206 329 4736 / momoseattle.com / Open daily

For some time now, the "in crowd" has been heading to this hood for design, food and fashion. Smack-dab in the center of it all sits MOMO. It doesn't matter whether or not you know "momo" means "peach" in Japanese, or that, like the store's motto, peaches signify a long and happy life. All you need to know is that this shop is where East meets West, and inside it's a happy explosion of colors, patterns and traditions. Irresistible Lorenzo Uomo socks from Italy; gorgeous Me & Arrow crop tops from LA; dazzling furoshiki fabric squares from Tokyo – MOMO has you covered from head to toe.

NORTHWEST TOFU

Cantonese-style eats in a factory

1913 South Jackson Street (near 20th Avenue South)
+1 206 328 8320 / No website / Closed Wednesday

Just getting inside a dim sum eatery in Seattle can be a competitive sport. You often have to battle it out for that elusive parking spot, jostle in line with others and – once you're seated – exercise your lightning-fast reflexes to reach the cart as it whizzes by. Or, you can relax and leisurely order dumplings and steamed buns at Northwest Tofu, a food manufacturer with an on-site eating house. Considering they spend hours every day making their own beancurd, noodles, yóutiáo (Chinese crullers) and soy milk, you know the ingredients are going to be fresh. I swing by for their deep-fried salt-and-pepper tofu – it's legendary. Granted, that doesn't mean you should shy away from the preserved thousand-year-old egg with pork and tofu.

SEATTLE PINBALL MUSEUM

Get ready to play

508 Maynard Avenue South (near South King Street)
+1 206 623 0759 / seattlepinballmuseum.com / Closed Tuesday

It would be easy to quote The Who's "Pinball Wizard" when describing this hangout, but that wouldn't do the place justice. With more than 40 vintage and modern pinball machines lining the walls, they offer not only the chance to drop a couple of quarters on your old favorites, but also host repair classes, special release parties and tournaments. Their oldest working machine, Texan, dates back to 1960, but you can also find the 1937 Nippy on display. Additionally, there's the limited edition America's Most Haunted, and the recently released The Big Lebowski game. This hands-on emporium will definitely bring out the kid in you.

TRICHOME

Head shop with well-designed wares

**618 South Jackson Street (near 6th Avenue South) / +1 206 905 9884
trichomeseattle.com / Open Wednesday through Sunday, Monday and
Tuesday by appointment**

The first time I stopped by Trichome, rowdy Seahawks fans were streaming
by on their way to the football stadium several blocks away. Inside,
the vibe was undeniably chill. That's because shop owners John Le and
Richard Saguin have created a space that is all about lifestyle and fashion,
where everyone is made to feel like a member of the Trichome community.
You'll find designer-made threads, accessories and home goods, like the
latest in elevated glassware, as well as cannabis culture gear. Check out the
stylistically restrained Tranzmission crew-neck sweater with printed elbow
patches or go bold with a graphic C.E. Empt-Ness shirt.

TSUKUSHINBO

Traditional Japanese family restaurant

515 South Main Street (near 6th Avenue South) / +1 206 467 4004
No website / Open daily

This hip Japanese eatery tucked into a nondescript building in the ID is where discerning locals have flocked for two decades. The matriach is the head chef who cooks up the tempting katsu curry donburi; the son knocks out sushi, sashimi and an assortment of rolls behind the sushi bar; and the daughter is the manager and runs the front of house. On Fridays, there's a noodle bowl special, where shoyu (soy sauce) ramen is the star of the show. Seattleites are for sure in the know about this delicious joint – you should be, too.

VENUS KARAOKE

Belt one out

601 South King Street, Suite 102 (near 6th Avenue South)
+1 206 264 1779 / venusktv.com / Open daily

We all have our signature songs – the ones that you can nail like a pro when you sing them in the shower or while driving down the highway alone in your car. I certainly have mine. But when you feel the urge to take the mic and strut your stuff on a bigger stage, grab a few friends and head to Venus Karaoke. Heck, grab as many friends as you'd like, as Venus has rooms large enough to accommodate 20 wannabe pop and rock stars. Their multi-language music selection changes as quickly as today's Top 40 while still paying respect to the classics.

WING LUKE MUSEUM OF THE ASIAN PACIFIC AMERICAN EXPERIENCE

An engaging, immersive, multicultural experience

719 South King Street (near Canton Alley South) / +1 206 623 5124
wingluke.org / Closed Monday

Wing Luke Museum isn't simply an arts space displaying the culture
and arts of Asian-Pacific Americans. Named after the first Asian-American
man elected to public office in the Pacific Northwest, the museum mounts
rotating, community-driven exhibits rooted in inspiring storytelling to bring
Asian-Pacific American culture, art and voices to the masses. Shows are
presented both inside and outside the stunning three-level facility.
The recent exhibition about Bruce Lee included photos, videos and
personal artifacts that showcased not only his impact in film, but
also how he handled racial stereotypes at that time. To make things
interactive, docents provided a guided tour through Chinatown,
where Lee spent his formative years. Other recent topics presented
have been works by Khmer Americans, and a show highlighting the
importance of tattoos in South Pacific Islander and Filipino cultures.

SEATTLE AFTER DARK:
raising the bar

Pinkies out

CANON WHISKEY AND BITTERS EMPORIUM

BATHTUB GIN & CO

2205 2nd Avenue (near Blanchard Street; Belltown)
+1 206 728 6069, bathtubginseattle.com, open daily

CANON WHISKEY AND BITTERS EMPORIUM

928 12th Avenue (near East Spring Street;
International District), no phone, canonseattle.com
open daily

FOREIGN NATIONAL

300 East Pike Street (near Bellevue Avenue;
Capitol Hill), +1 206 557 7273, foreignnationalbar.com
open daily

HEARTWOOD PROVISIONS

1103 1st Avenue (near Spring Street; Downtown)
+1 206 582 3505, heartwoodsea.com, open daily

ROB ROY

2332 2nd Avenue (near Battery Street; Belltown)
+1 206 956 8423, robroyseattle.com, open daily

TAVERN LAW

1406 12th Avenue (near East Madison Street;
Capitol Hill), +1 206 322 9734, tavernlaw.com
open daily

There's no question that Seattleites have an affinity for their $2 Rainier tallboys. That said, look around and you'll see that the craft booze craze has taken hold, and there's no denying that we pine for our whiskey, rye and rum.

With more than 3,500 labels staring at you from behind the bar, you won't have any difficulty landing on a spirit of choice at **Canon Whiskey and Bitters Emporium**. They boast the largest whiskey collection in the entire Western Hemisphere and proffer flights such as the Smoke Bomb – pours of Ardbeg, Laphroaig and Lagavulin. Antique glassware, comfy leather booths and bespoke concoctions: Canon is a class act.

A recent newcomer on the Downtown scene, **Heartwood Provisions** has already won over many in this city. It could be their cocktails, which they expertly pair with your dinner, or perhaps it's the fresh, seasonal juices and aromatics reflecting Pacific Northwest sensibilities that are found behind the bar. Sip on snap pea juice with gin or kick back with some cachaça laced with a strawberry-lavender-sage syrup.

There's a not-so-secret secret about **Tavern Law**. Pick up the old-school phone that's located on the wall and there's a chance you'll be invited upstairs to their speakeasy, Needle & Thread, which specializes in Prohibition-Era libations. Even if the space is booked, you're still in luck: Tavern Law's main bar is as spacious as its hooch list is extensive, and they've been known to take craft tipples to the next level by mixing up custom beverages on request. My usual is the Concealed Weapon: Ardberg Ten Years Old, Fino and Amaro Nardini liqueur.

Walking into **Foreign National**, a dimly lit enclave of a bar, is like finding yourself in an entirely different country. This joint will intoxicate you with its intimacy and have your senses swirling along with the disco ball that hangs in the corner. Or it could be their signature drink with pisco and Amaro Montenegro.

As a Midwesterner, I'm prone to striking up conversations with strangers. Years ago, one such conversation led me to the then-brand spankin' new drinking lounge, **Bathtub Gin & Co**. Hidden in an alley in Belltown, this pint-sized, Prohibition-themed watering hole serves an impressive array of gins and the crave-worthy Death Star, made with bourbon, fig and maple syrup.

Belltown is also home to **Rob Roy**, a top pick not only among thirsty denizens, but also many of the hardworking barkeeps around the city. For more than 15 years, owner and bartender Anu Elford has been providing us all with a welcoming sanctuary to unwind at the end of the day — nestle into one of their leather sofas while sipping a superbly executed Old Fashioned.

SEATTLE AFTER DARK:
to the stage

Here we are now, entertain us

12TH AVENUE ARTS
1620 12th Avenue (near East Pine Street;
Capitol Hill), no phone, blackboxoperations.org
check website for performance schedule

CENTURY BALLROOM
915 East Pine Street (at Nagle Place; Capitol Hill)
+1 206 324 7263, centuryballroom.com, open daily

LO-FI PERFORMANCE GALLERY
429 Eastlake Avenue (near Republican Street;
Capitol Hill), + 1 206 254 2824, thelofi.net, open daily

THE COMEDY UNDERGROUND
109 South Washington Street (near 1st Avenue South)
+1 206 628 0303, comedyunderground.com
open daily

THE RENDEZVOUS AND JEWELBOX THEATER
2322 2nd Avenue (near Battery Street; Belltown)
+1 206 441 5823, therendezvous.rocks, open daily

TRACTOR TAVERN
5213 Ballard Avenue Northwest (near 20th Avenue
Northwest; Ballard), +1 206 789 3599
tractortavern.com, open daily

Grunge — remember that? We have so moved on since then. You still might see an occasional flannel shirt here and there, but the music, theater and live performance scene in Seattle has left the '90s behind and is not looking back.

It may only have two stages, but **12th Avenue Arts** sure knows how to make the most of them. With more than two dozen of the most inventive and relevant theater groups sharing the space and creating often courageous work — from modern takes on Shakespeare to newer plays like *The Motherf***er with the Hat* by Stephen Adly Guirgis — 12th Avenue Arts is definitely the place to be.

Ellen DeGeneres, Louis C.K., Rosie O'Donnell and Jerry Seinfeld may be household names today, but when these comedians stopped by **The Comedy Underground**, they were up-and-comers waiting for their big break. There are a lot of outstanding comedians waiting to hit it big, and this is the premier place in town to discover them.

In a somewhat industrial area of South Lake Union, **LO-FI Performance Gallery** refuses to give up the night. Here, bands and DJs play punk, rock and electronica to the energetic crowds. If full-on frenzy isn't your scene, stop by for soul night, when things seem to take on their own special groove, or head to the back where a few arcade games live.

TRACTOR TAVERN

You never know what you might find when you drop by
The Rendezvous and Jewelbox Theater. Comedy, films, plays, burlesque
and cabaret shows hit the stage on any given night. Past the main bar,
there's the petite Jewelbox Theater that's been lovingly restored to its
1932 splendor and puts you in the mood for a night out.

Got a swing in your step? Head to **Century Ballroom**. Beginner or pro,
you'll always be welcomed with open arms. Show up an hour early for a wallet-
friendly intro dance lesson if your moves are a little rusty, then stick around for
the free salsa, swing and bachata sessions.

A no-nonsense music venue, **Tractor Tavern** has been serving up alt country,
folk and a little bit of southern rock 'n' roll thrown in for good measure for the
past 20 years. Aching to get out on the floor for a little two-stepping? Come by
for their weekly Monday night square dance party, where callers will help you
through the moves.

georgetown

beacon hill, columbia city

On your way to the top of Beacon Hill, you'll run
across an unparalleled view overlooking the city at
Dr. Jose Rizal Park. On the other end of the area is
the largest Olmsted-planned green space in Seattle –
Jefferson Park. That's not to suggest Beacon Hill is one
big pastoral playground. The community has always had
juice: hip-hop, rap, R&B and spoken word artists have
called it home for decades, and now the rest of the city
seems to be moving in and playing catch-up. Just south,
the mostly residential Columbia City boasts destination-
worthy shops and restaurants along a few short blocks of
Rainier Avenue, and a quick hop across I-5 will bring you
to Georgetown. Arguably Seattle's oldest neighborhood,
it remains steadfast in an area known for its aviation and
industrial roots. These days, you'll see hipsters mingling
right alongside old-timers in the repurposed warehouses
and long-standing saloons.

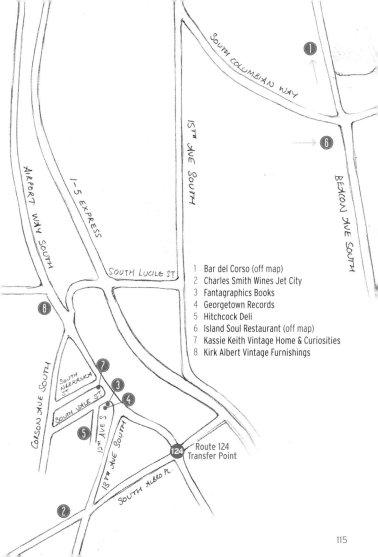

SOUTH COLUMBIAN WAY

15TH AVE SOUTH

BEACON AVE SOUTH

AIRPORT WAY SOUTH

I-5 EXPRESS

SOUTH LUCILE ST

CARSON AVE SOUTH

SOUTH NEBRASKA ST

SOUTH VALE ST

12TH AVE S

13TH AVE SOUTH

SOUTH ALBRO PL.

Route 124
Transfer Point

1 Bar del Corso (off map)
2 Charles Smith Wines Jet City
3 Fantagraphics Books
4 Georgetown Records
5 Hitchcock Deli
6 Island Soul Restaurant (off map)
7 Kassie Keith Vintage Home & Curiosities
8 Kirk Albert Vintage Furnishings

BAR DEL CORSO

Toothsome Italian fare

3057 Beacon Avenue South (near South Hanford Street)
+1 206 395 2069 / bardelcorso.com / Closed Sunday and Monday

Each time I travel to Italy, I inevitably wonder what it would be like to put down roots there. The Italians' love of life, language and food always has me planning my return visit the moment I step foot stateside. Until then, I frequent Bar del Corso – a fantastic place that has all of those Italian qualities to hold me over until my next transatlantic trip. The warm and inviting room, the Neapolitan pizzas with cremini mushrooms and housemade sausage, the grilled octopus and the olive oil-braised pork shoulder remind me of that Italian proverb, "live to eat, not eat to live". Buon appetito!

CHARLES SMITH WINES JET CITY

Urban winery

1136 South Albro Place (near 13th Avenue South) / +1 206 745 7456
charlessmithwines.com / Closed Monday and Tuesday

I've been to my fair share of wineries over the years. Tasting a vintage while overlooking rolling hills with the resident dog snoozing at your feet is not a bad way to spend an afternoon – but sometimes you just have to mix things up. Sitting in a former 32,000-sq.ft. Dr Pepper bottling plant, tasting award-winning labels while watching planes touch down at Boeing Field, is what I call wine with an attitude – in the best possible way. From his K Vintners River Rock Syrah to his ViNO Rosé, Charles Smith makes wines that are accessible, affordable and, most importantly, delicious.

FANTAGRAPHICS BOOKS

Artistic tomes

**1201 South Vale Street (at Airport Way South) / +1 206 658 0110
fantagraphics.com / Open daily**

Whoever said comic books were just for kids has obviously never been to
Fantagraphics Books. A trove of some of the most celebrated cartoonists
assembled in one place, this shop has shelves lined with all kinds of graphic
works, 'zines and collections of classic strips that will appeal to the adult
sensibilities in all of us. The illustrated history of punk rock lives right
alongside a complete volume of *Peanuts*, simultaneously capturing the
imagination of several generations of cartoon fans. If you've ever thumbed
through a comic with fascination and admiration of the storyline and art
form, then this is your holy grail.

GEORGETOWN RECORDS

Diggers' delight

1201 South Vale Street (at Airport Way South) / +1 206 762 5638
georgetownrecords.net / Open daily

Whenever I'm in the neighborhood, I always find myself making my way
to Georgetown Records – whether I'm in the market for music or not.
I'm usually already hanging at Fantagraphics Books (see pg 118), so I don't
have to travel too far as they share the same front door. Soul, country, punk,
post-punk, new wave, world music, progressive jazz and some genres that
defy categorization are at your fingertips here. There's a cool vibe that
brings out a posse of music lovers from all over the city looking to get
their vinyl fix. On my most recent trip, I walked away with Nina Simone,
C'est Chic and Hank Williams. See what I mean?

HITCHCOCK DELI

Damn good eats

**6003 12th Avenue South (near South Vale Street) / +1 206 582 2796
hitchcockdeli.com / Open daily**

We might be 3,000 miles from New York City, but doesn't mean we can't have a decent pastrami sandwich. In fact, thanks to chef and owner Brendan McGill, we can get a rather fine one. This sucker comes with raw sauerkraut that's fermented on premise – like all of the other condiments and preserves they serve up. Load up with an entire pound of pastrami if you want your sandwich New York-style. Corned beef brisket, thick-sliced porchetta and smoked ham with triple-crème brie are equal to the task and might even convince a New Yorker that the West Coast is the best coast.

ISLAND SOUL RESTAURANT

Fresh Jamaican fare

4869 Rainier Avenue South (near South Ferdinand Street) / +1 206 329 1202 islandsoulrestaurant.net / Open daily

Sometimes, what my day needs is a bit of paradise. A place where I can unwind and feel as if I'm on island time. When the mood strikes, I drop by this little slice of Caribbean heaven, which has all the tastes of the tropics I so desire. Fruity rum drinks? Check. Snapper with red beans and rice? Yes, please. Chef Bobby hails from Jamaica, and there's no doubt that he certainly knows his way around the jerk spices. Add a little reggae, some inspired art and a commanding portrait of Bob Marley into the mix, and before you know it, you'll be swaying to "One Love" and time will suddenly be the furthest thing from your mind.

KASSIE KEITH VINTAGE HOME & CURIOSITIES

Curated housewares

5951 Airport Way South (near South Nebraska Street)
+1 206 420 3158 / kassiekeith.com / Closed Monday and Tuesday

I can't remember the last time I needed a pair of oversized cast iron spurs. Should the need ever arise, I'm heading straight to Kassie Keith Vintage Home & Curiosities. You never know what you're going to run across when you hunt through the aisles of this divine boutique filled with antiques and objects of eras gone by. The staff is always easy-going and willing to share the stories behind their eccentric finds, which means you'll walk away with a Victorian deer antler shaving stand thinking it's one of the most reasonable things you've ever purchased.

KIRK ALBERT
VINTAGE FURNISHINGS

Hard-to-find and custom design

5517 Airport Way South (near South Lucile Street) / +1 206 762 3899
kirkalbert.com / Open Wednesday through Saturday

There was a time when I would scour secondhand stores and estate sales to find that matchless piece of furniture. More often than not, I would pick up an object that needed just a little TLC, which meant a project that may – or may not – get completed. Now I head to Kirk Albert's showroom, where he has the knack of unearthing stunning, original finds from his travels abroad and putting his own finishing touches on them, saving me from yet another to-do on my project list. Whether it's an old-school slate chalkboard or a European wall-mounted slot machine, there's a good chance you'll find it here.

get outside

Urban natural beauty

DISCOVERY PARK

From theaters and museums to shopping and dining, this city has plenty of activities that can keep you indoors all day. But part of Seattle's draw lies away from the concrete jungle. Venture out and feel the grass under your feet. Mother Nature awaits.

You only have to travel five miles northwest of downtown to find yourself in the largest green space in the city – **Discovery Park**. Here, you can hike the trails through open meadowlands and forest groves, make your way to the shores of Puget Sound and walk the beach to the lighthouse while bald eagles soar overhead.

Looking for a little exercise? A favorite among walkers, runners and cyclists, the **Burke-Gilman Trail** stretches 27 miles from east to west. Urban to suburban to lakefront, this path offers an abundance of views.

With all of the water surrounding this city, it would be a shame not to get out on it. Head to **The Center for Wooden Boats** and rent a canoe, kayak, rowboat or other seafaring vessel, and skim the waters of Lake Union. Their Public Sunday Sail is a terrific way to board a classic wooden sailboat and have an experienced skipper navigate you through the houseboats, landing seaplanes and working shipyards.

Hugging the shores of Lake Washington, **Washington Park Arboretum** spans 230 acres where gardens, wetlands and walking trails showcase some of the most diverse plants in North America. The Seattle Japanese Garden, located within the Arboretum, is one of the most highly regarded grounds of its kind around.

Prefer to get your fresh air downtown? Hop on over to the **Olympic Sculpture Park**. Rising 40 feet from the waterfront, it features some amazing, unobstructed vistas of Elliott Bay and the Olympic Mountains. It's an excellent place for a picnic as you take in large sculptures from well-known artists like Alexander Calder, Richard Serra and Louise Bourgeois.

BURKE-GILMAN TRAIL
Golden Gardens Park to Sammamish River Trail
(Ballard to Bothell), +1 206 684 7583
seattle.gov/transportation/BGT.htm, open daily

DISCOVERY PARK
3801 Discovery Park Boulevard
(near 36th Avenue West; Lawtonwood)
+1 206 386 4236, seattle.gov/parks, open daily

OLYMPIC SCULPTURE PARK
2901 Western Avenue (near Broad Street; Belltown)
+1 206 654 3100, seattleartmuseum.org/visit/
olympic-sculpture-park, open daily

THE CENTER FOR WOODEN BOATS
1010 Valley Street (along Cheshiahud Lake Union
Loop; South Lake Union), +1 206 382 2628, cwb.org/
locations/south-lake-union, closed Tuesday

WASHINGTON PARK ARBORETUM
2300 Arboretum Drive East (near East Foster
Island Road; Montlake), +1 206 543 8616
depts.washington.edu/wpa, open daily